CARTOONS 2021, 2022 & 2023

DR. YADUVIR SINGH

Made with ♥ on the Notion Press Platform
www.notionpress.com

The Book, "Cartoons 2021, 2022 & 2023" is dedicated to the God, with a passionate prayer for complete well-being of the whole humanity and the entire creation.

Contents

Contents

Contents

Foreword

The impressive and involving Cartoon Book, "Cartoons 2021, 2022 & 2023" has covered nearly all major events in a very humorous style and satires, which had become highlights in the years, viz. 2021 partially, 2022 and 2023 full. These events included Petrol and Diesel price hike, AICTE decision, First Anniversary of COVID - 19, Oxygen Express, Price Inflation, Tokyo 2020 Olympics, Purchase of Air India by Tata, Farmers Laws in India, Miss 2021 Pageant, Union Budget 2022, Assembly Elections 2022 in Indian States, Pakistan Political Crisis, Maharashtra State Government Debacle, Cheetah arriving from Namibia to India, India hosting G20 Summit, FIFA World Cup Qatar 2022, Joshimath Landslide in India, Rahul Gandhi Cross - Country Yatra, Hindenburg Report, Rahul Gandhi expulsion from Indian Parliament, Wrestlers Protest in India, Arrest of Mr. Imran Khan Former Prime Minister of Pakistan, India - USA GE 414 Jet Engine Deal, Launch of Chandrayaan - 3 Spacecraft, 2023 Israel - Hamas War, 2023 Uttarakhand Tunnel Collapse in India etc.. Cartoons are for everybody. Cartoons are the smartest way of communication - reporting, appreciating and criticising, without annoying anybody. Cartoons are joys of life. This Book will also educate the Art of Cartoon Sketching, Theme Representation and Expression. This Book will take the readers to the memories of the past. Events are over, but their memories last forever, and eventually, become part of the life. Life brings tears, smiles, pains, comforts, failures, success, loss, gain, and finally, memories are created. This Book, through its satirical cartoons, will turn reader' tears into smiles. Cartoons ate colours, music, smiles, joys, peace and happiness of the life.

Author's attempt of publishing this Cartoon Book, "Cartoons 2021, 2022 & 2023", apart from his several other highly successful books and best sellers from Life Engineering (Spirituality), is worth appreciating. Bringing a smile on the face is one of the greatest jobs, which only a few blessed beings can do, on this planet. Kudos to the author, for this marvellous creation, i.e. the Cartoon Book, "Cartoons 2021, 2022 & 2023".

- **Baba**

Place: Baba Niwas, India
Date: 22 / 03 / 2024

Preface

Cartoons are the joys of the life. Cartoons have multiple interpretations. A reader or a viewer has his or her own interpretation about the cartoon, may be totally different from that of the cartoonist, but laughs after seeing the cartoon. Cartoon is a subtle and smartest way of sending message(s), or making an efficient communication, without hurting the character(s) depicted in the cartoon, and the reader. Cartoon is a graphical language of communication. After the well known five senses of the beings, viz. eyes, nose, tongue, ears and the skin, sixth sense the inner voice or the gut feeling or the hunch, seventh sense the uncommon common sense, is the eighth sense, the sense of humour. Cartoon is the humour. Humour is the gift of the God to the beings for leading a happy and a joyful physical life. Cartoons are for everybody. Cartoons are the smartest way of communication without annoying anybody.

This Cartoon Book, "Cartoons 2021, 2022 & 2023" covers nearly all major events in a very humorous style and satires, which had become highlights in the years, viz. 2021 partially, 2022 and 2023 full. These events included Petrol and Diesel price hike, AICTE decision, First Anniversary of COVID - 19, Oxygen Express, Price Inflation, Tokyo 2020 Olympics, Purchase of Air India by Tata, Farmers Laws in India, Miss 2021 Pageant, Union Budget 2022, Assembly Elections 2022 in Indian States, Pakistan Political Crisis, Maharashtra State Government Debacle, Cheetah arriving from Namibia to India, India hosting G20 Summit, FIFA World Cup Qatar 2022, Joshimath Landslide in India, Rahul Gandhi Cross - Country Yatra, Hindenburg Report, Rahul

Gandhi expulsion from Indian Parliament, Wrestlers Protest in India, Arrest of Mr. Imran Khan Former Prime Minister of Pakistan, India - USA GE 414 Jet Engine Deal, Launch of Chandrayaan - 3 Spacecraft, 2023 Israel - Hamas War, 2023 Uttarakhand Tunnel Collapse in India etc..

This Cartoon Book, "Cartoons 2021, 2022 & 2023" will also educate the art of cartoon sketching, and theme representation and expression. This Cartoon Book, "Cartoons 2021, 2022 & 2023" will take the reader to the memories of the past of years 2021, 2022 and 2023. Events are over, but their memories last forever, and eventually become the part of the life journey. Life brings tears, smiles, and creates the memories. This Cartoon Book, "Cartoons 2021, 2022 & 2023", through its satirical and hilarious cartoons, will surely turn the reader's tears if any, into smiles, and sorrows if any, into joys.

- Dr. Yaduvir Singh

Country: India
Date: 25 / 02 / 2024

Acknowledgements

The Cartoonist of this Cartoon Book, "Cartoons 2021, 2022 & 2023" will like to acknowledge all sources of news, viz. TV Channels, Newspapers, Websites, Social Media Platforms etc., for providing the information about the events, which happened in the years 2021, 2022 and 2023. The Cartoonist of this Cartoon Book, "Cartoons 2021, 2022 & 2023" will like to tender his sincere apologies in anticipation, for having hurt the sentiments, views, persona, image, character etc. of being(s), group (s), society(s), state(s), nation(s) etc., depicted here, if any, as it will be sheer coincidental and inadvertent on the part of the Cartoonist. Cartoons are meant for the purpose of positive recreation, and directed towards the views and thoughts of a considerate and tolerant society. Readers and Viewers may have a totally different view and opinion of what is being expressed here through the sketched cartoons. Readers and Viewers discretion and openness of mind is pleaded / solicited.

Prologue

The Cartoon Book, "Cartoons 2021, 2022 & 2023" is a gem book, and a worthy collection. Laughing is the best exercise and therapy. Life is meant for celebration. The Cartoon Book, "Cartoons 2021, 2022 & 2023" is a rare book. This Cartoon Book, "Cartoons 2021, 2022 & 2023", through its satirical and humourous cartoons will turn reader's /viewer's tears into smiles. Cartoons are the colours, music, smiles, joys and the happiness of life. Cartoons are smartest way of communication without annoying any being. The Cartoon Book, "Cartoons 2021, 2022 & 2023" has covered nearly all prominent events of years 2021, 2022 and 2023 in a very humourous style, using satires. These events included Petrol and Diesel price hike, AICTE decision, First Anniversary of COVID - 19, Oxygen Express, Price Inflation, Tokyo 2020 Olympics, Purchase of Air India by Tata, Farmers Laws in India, Miss 2021 Pageant, Union Budget 2022, Assembly Elections 2022 in Indian States, Pakistan Political Crisis, Maharashtra State Government Debacle, Cheetah arriving from Namibia to India, India hosting G20 Summit, FIFA World Cup Qatar 2022, Joshimath Landslide in India, Rahul Gandhi Cross - Country Yatra, Hindenburg Report, Rahul Gandhi expulsion from Indian Parliament, Wrestlers Protest in India, Arrest of Mr. Imran Khan Former Prime Minister of Pakistan, India - USA GE 414 Jet Engine Deal, Launch of Chandrayaan - 3 Spacecraft, 2023 Israel - Hamas War, 2023 Uttarakhand Tunnel Collapse in India etc.. This Cartoon Book, "Cartoons 2021, 2022 & 2023" is a tool for self-help, in order to remain happy, smile and laugh, and also, to make others happy, smile and laugh. Cartoons are for everybody.

CHAPTER ONE

Petrol And Diesel Prices Touching Rs. 100.00 Per Litre

Petrol and Diesel prices touching Rs. 100.00 per litre

This cartoon was sketched on 26 February, 2021. Petrol and Diesel prices had skyrocketed, and were touching Rs. 100.00 per litre. There were countrywide protests over it.

CHAPTER TWO

AICTE Makes PCM Non-Compulsory For Engineering Courses

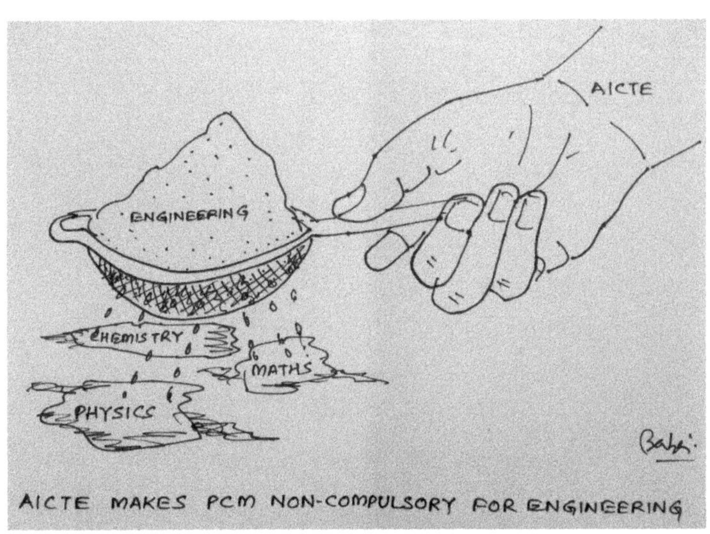

AICTE makes PCM non-compulsory for engineering courses

This cartoon was sketched on 17 March, 2021. All India Council of Technical Education (AICTE) had announced that subjects Physics, Chemistry and Mathematics (PCM) at 10+2 level (entry level for engineering) are not compulsory for engineering courses.

CHAPTER THREE

First Anniversary Of COVID-19

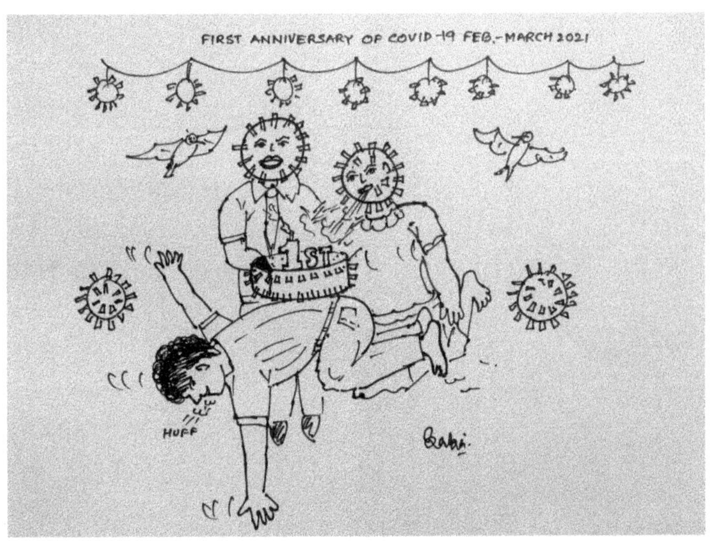

Corona viruses celebrating first anniversary

This cartoon was sketched on 26 March, 2021. It is more than a year as of now, but Corona is still existing and swallowing the humanity. It is being reported on TV channels, and also, in the newspapers that Corona virus is mutating itself, and developing its new strains. Despite Corona vaccine in the market, and people getting vaccinated also, Corona disease is still spreading.

CHAPTER FOUR

Container Ship "Ever Given" Stuck In Suez Canal

Container Ship "Ever Given" Stuck In Suez Canal

This cartoon was sketched on 31 March, 2021. It was reported on 29 March, 2021 that a container ship named as "Ever Given" got stuck in Suez Canal in Egypt. After approximately a weeklong efforts, with the help of many tugboats, this ship could be straightened, and finally slipped onto the sea. It caused a great loss of commerce, as many other cargo ships kept waiting for its clearance. Around 15 % of global trade is shipped through Suez Canal.

CHAPTER FIVE

Corona Cases On All Time High

Corona cases on all time high

This cartoon was sketched on 9 April, 2021. Corona cases have been told on TV and radio to be all time high so far, with 1,20,000+ daily cases in India, in the month of April, 2021.

CHAPTER SIX

The Oxygen Express In India

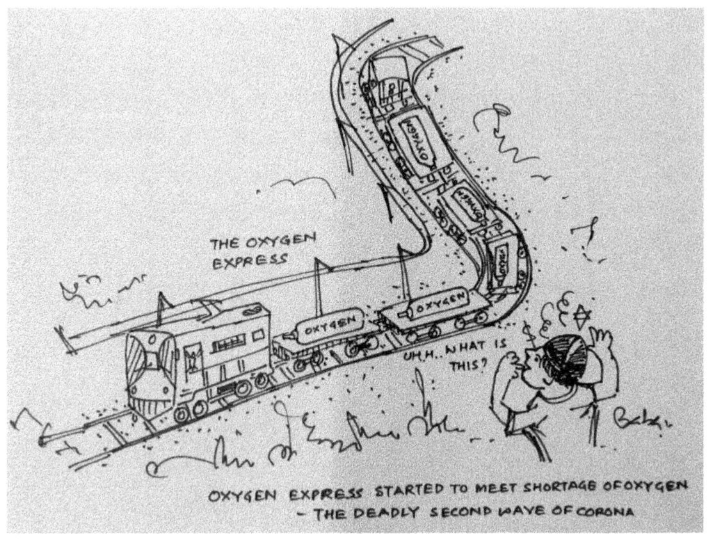

The Oxygen Express in India

This cartoon was sketched on 23 April, 2021. There was an acute shortage of Oxygen for ICU admitted Corona patients in the hospitals in almost all the cities of India.

There were no beds in the hospitals. There had been a sudden burst of new Corona patients. Per day Corona infection had even crossed 3.25 Lakhs mark in India. Indian medical infrastructure had come on knees and crumbled. Hoarding and black marketing of vaccines and other needed medicines had started. There was shortage of the needed medicines. It was a worst, pathetic and hopeless situation, seen so far, by me in my life. There was a complete despair, dejection and melancholy all over among all the people of India. People had been living under a constant fear of death. Truly, it was a punishment inflicted on mankind by the nature. People had been dying in large numbers due to breathlessness. Infection had reached their lungs. There were no spaces left in the graveyards to bury the dead bodies, and also, there were long queues in the cremation grounds to crenate the dead bodies. To meet shortage of supply of Oxygen, the government had started few Oxygen Express trains. People had been looting Oxygen cylinders. Enormous security was put, and green corridors were created for safe, speedy and bulk transportation of Oxygen cylinders to the hospitals.

CHAPTER SEVEN

Triple Whammy

Triple Whammy - second wave COVID - 19, Tao Te Tufan and Yash Tufan

This cartoon was sketched on 28 May, 2021. It was a triple whammy. India was already facing challenges created due to second wave of COVID - 19. Then, Tao Te Tufan in Arabian Sea, and immediately after it, Yash Tufan in Bay of Bengal, all brought the country to knees. Salute to the human spirit to fight, endure and survive. Second wave of COVID - 19, and both Tufan has caused great loss of men, money, and materials.

CHAPTER EIGHT

Need Of Oxygen During Second Wave Of Corona In India

Need of Oxygen during second wave of Corona in India

This cartoon was sketched on 10 May, 2021. There was severe shortage of oxygen, ICU beds and medicine in the hospitals during the second wave of Corona in India. The cases of Corona infection were reported to be touching 4 Lakhs every day and were on constant rise in India. It was the worst time in human civilisation of current times.

CHAPTER NINE

The Big Fight - Ayurveda Versus Allopathy in India

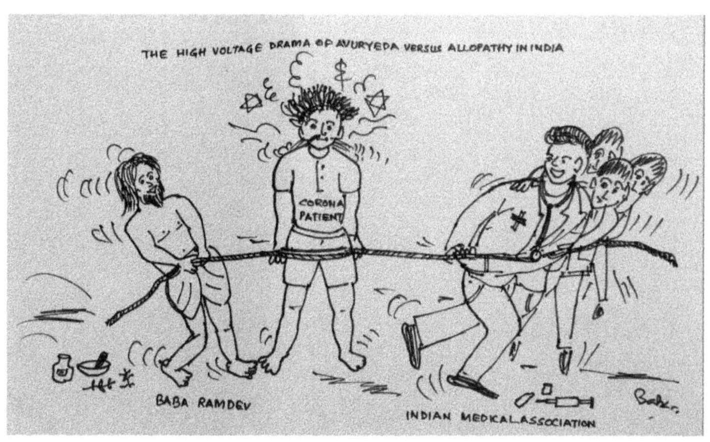

The high voltage drama of Ayurveda versus Allopathy in India

This cartoon was sketched on 4 June, 2021. Ayurveda is the traditional Hindu system of medicine with historical roots in the Indian subcontinent. Ayurveda uses a combination of diet, herbal treatment, and yogic breathing to treat illnesses. Allopathy is treatment of disease by conventional means. Allopathy uses drugs having effects opposite to the symptoms. The proponent of Ayurveda in India, Baba Ramdev commented that more deaths of Corona patients have happened due to Allopathic treatments. He commented that Allopathic doctors are dying in large numbers, and are unable to cure the Corona patients. Baba Ramdev said that Allopathy is a failure. Indian Medical Association (IMA) and various other associations of Allopathic doctors in India opposed it vehemently, made its complaint with the government, and also, took the matter to the court. Despite Baba Ramdev's apologies and public withdrawal of his earlier comments, IMA is not relenting. Allopathic doctors labelled Ayurveda as a pseudoscience.

CHAPTER TEN

Price Inflation Monster

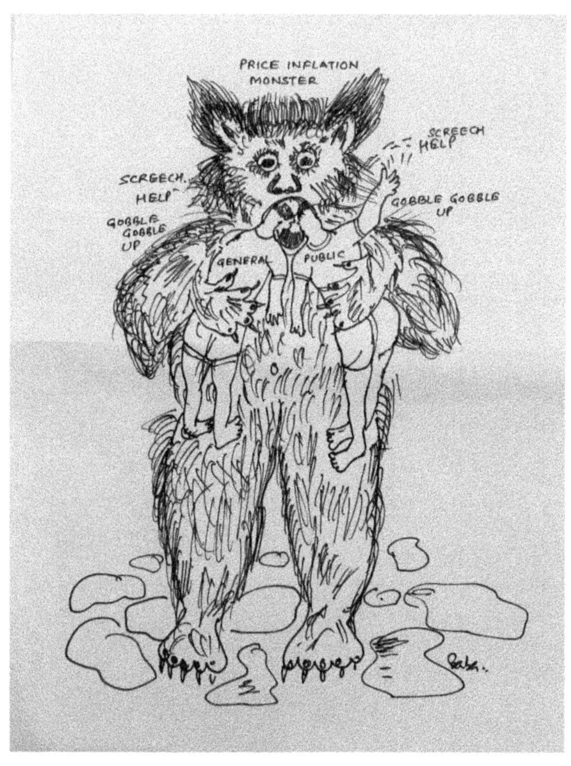

Price inflation monster

This cartoon was sketched on 18 June, 2021. The wholesale price inflation was all time high. People were in quandary. Price inflation monster was gobbling up the masses of the country.

CHAPTER ELEVEN

Scorching Heat Of June - July 2021

Scorching heat of June - July 2021

This cartoon was sketched on 07 July, 2021. There was intense heat and hot wave in the north and central India especially, as reported. It had broken records of many years in the past.

CHAPTER TWELVE

Hum Do, Hamaare Do - We Two, Our Two

Hum Do, Hamaare Do - We Two, Our Two

This cartoon was sketched on 20 July, 2021. On World Population Day, the Chief Minister of Uttar Pradesh, a state in India, said that bringing "Hum Do, Hamaare Do" bill is necessary to control and stabilize the population, in order to promote sustainable development with equitable distribution of available wealth and resources.

CHAPTER THIRTEEN

Pride Of India

Pride of India

This was sketched on 4 August, 2021. P. V. Sindhu had won a bronze medal in women's singles badminton in Olympics 2020 held in Tokyo, Japan. Mirabai Chanu Saikhom had won a silver medal in women's 49 kg weightlifting. Lovlina Borgohain had won a bronze medal in women's welterweight boxing. Many other sportspersons had also won medal for India. These sportspersons are pride of India.

CHAPTER FOURTEEN

Neeraj Chopra - Golden Boy Of India

Neeraj Chopra - Golden Boy of India

This was sketched on 11 August, 2021. Neeraj Chopra had won a gold medal in men's javelin throw, an athletics event, held in Olympics 2020 in Tokyo, Japan. It was the highest ever score of medals in Olympics games of India. With seven medals, viz. one gold medal, two silver medals and four bronze medals, the Tokyo 2020 Olympics has been the most decorated Olympic Games in India's history. India has now surpassed its previous best of 6 medals from the London Olympics Games in 2012. Javelin thrower Neeraj Chopra has entered India's history book by delivering a first-ever Olympic track-and-field event gold medal. Before Neeraj Chopra, the only medal that India had won in track-and-field events was back in 1900, when British-Indian Norman Pritchard had won two silver medals in Paris Olympics. So, it was a medal won again after 121 years in a track-and-field event in Olympics for India. Neeraj Chopra also became first Indian to win an individual Olympic gold in track-and-field event, post-independence. Late Milkha Singh (20 November 1929 – 18 June 2021), also known as "The Flying Sikh", was an Indian track-and-field sprinter, who had represented India in the 1956 Summer Olympics in Melbourne, the 1960 Summer Olympics in Rome and the 1964 Summer Olympics in Tokyo. Late Milkha Singh came very close to win an Olympic medal in the 1960 Games, only to finish 4th in the final of men's 400 meters. PT Usha was in great form heading into the 1984 Games, but she also missed out on a bronze medal by 0.01 seconds in the women's 400 meters hurdles. Neeraj Chopra fulfilled legendary Milkha Singh's dream by winning a Gold medal in track and field at the Olympics. Neeraj Chopra dedicated his Olympics gold medal to Milkha Singh and PT Usha.

CHAPTER FIFTEEN

The Great 2021 Siege Of Afghanistan By Taliban

2021 Afghanistan siege by Taliban

This cartoon was sketched on 21 August, 2021. The 2021 Taliban offensive was the final major offensive by the Taliban and its other allied militant groups against the Islamic Republic of Afghanistan. It began on 1 May 2021, coinciding with the withdrawal of most of the United States and allied troops from Afghanistan. It resulted in de facto takeover of the country by the Taliban, and the reinstatement of the Islamic Emirate of Afghanistan.

CHAPTER SIXTEEN

India Crosses One Crore A Day Corona Jabs Mark

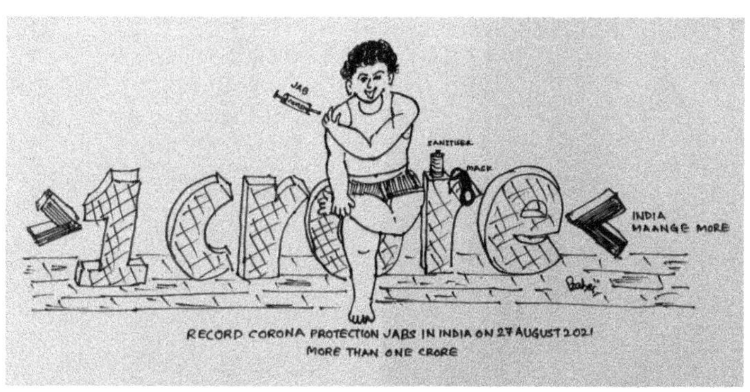

India crosses one crore a day Corona jabs mark

This cartoon was sketched on 28 August, 2021. India made a record of Corona jabs, crossing one crore mark on a single day on 27 August, 2021. As reported, 25.8% population was administered first dose, and 7.2%

population was fully vaccinated, by this date.

CHAPTER SEVENTEEN

India In Tokyo 2020 Paralympic Games

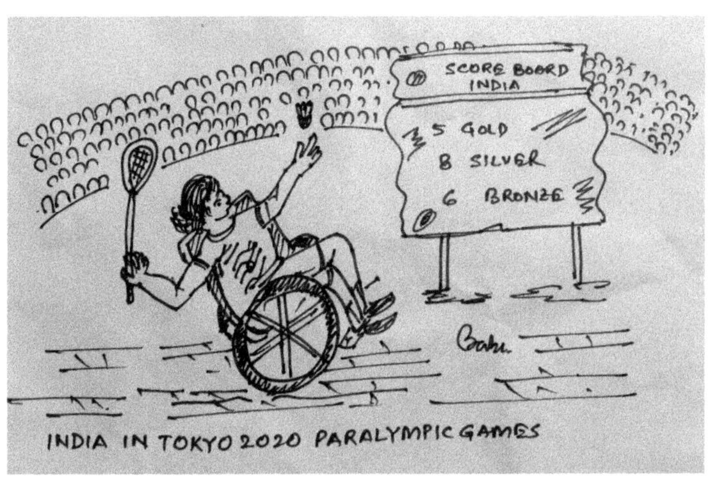

India in Tokyo 2020 Paralympic Games

This was sketched on 15 September, 2021. India had won 5 gold medals, 8 silver medals and 6 bronze medals in Tokyo 2020 Paralympic Games. Tokyo 2020 was India's best-ever Paralympics. Shooter Avani Lekhara became the first Indian woman to win two Paralympics medals. This haul had comfortably eclipsed India's previous best medals tallies of four each at the Stoke Mandeville and New York Games in 1984 and Rio 2016. The game of shooting for India had emerged as the biggest contributor of medals with five medals, followed by the game of high jump and the game of badminton with four medals each. There were several historic firsts to celebrate as well this time. Bhavina Patel became the first Indian table tennis player to win a Paralympic medal. Harvinder Singh mirrored the feat in archery. However, Shooter Avani Lekhara was the standout name. Avani Lekhara became the first Indian woman to win a Paralympic gold medal.

CHAPTER EIGHTEEN

Evergrande Crisis

Evergrande Crisis

This cartoon was sketched on 25 September, 2021. Chinese real estate major Evergrande was facing worst fund crunch. Markets were spooked with its adverse impacts on global economy. Economists had been asserting it to be another Lehman moment.

CHAPTER NINETEEN

Tata Buying Air India

Tata buying Air India

This cartoon was sketched on 13 October, 2021. Tata is buying Air India, and bringing it back to its portfolio, ever since it was nationalised in year 1953.

CHAPTER TWENTY

India Crosses Record 100 Crore COVID - 19 Vaccination Mark

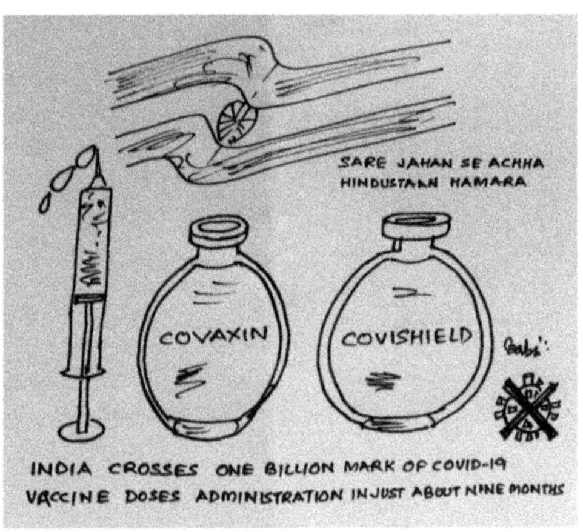

India crosses record 100 crore COVID - 19 vaccination mark

This was sketched on 29 October, 2021. India had completed record 100 crore doses of COVID - 19 vaccines on 21 October, 2021, in about 9 months since the vaccination drive began.

CHAPTER TWENTY-ONE

Delhi - Most Polluted City On The Earth

Delhi - most polluted city on the earth

This cartoon was sketched on 14 November, 2021. Delhi's Air Quality Index (AQI) had exceeded 462 mark, which is too dangerous. Everyday AQI is published by the state-run System of Air Quality and Weather Forecasting and Research (SAFAR). Readings below 50 are considered to be safe, while anything above 300 is considered to be hazardous or 'severe'. Post Deepawali, due to pollution of crackers burning and crop residue (straw / Parali) burning, Delhi was reduced into a gas chamber, causing its denizens problems of breathing, and itching and sore in the eyes.

CHAPTER TWENTY-TWO

PM Modi Withdrew The Three Farm Laws

PM Modi withdrew the three farm laws

This cartoon was sketched on 19 November, 2021. Indian Prime Minister Narendra Modi had announced the repeal of the three contentious farm laws. Farmers, mostly from the states of Punjab and Haryana, have been protesting against these three laws at the borders of Delhi since 26 November, 2020.

CHAPTER TWENTY-THREE

Miss Universe 2021 From India

Miss Universe 2021 - Ms. Harnaaz Kaur Sandhu from India

This was sketched on 18 December, 2021. Ms. Harnaaz Kaur Sandhu has won the title of Miss Universe 2021. She is the third Indian to win this prestigious and coveted title, after a long wait for twenty one years, after Ms. Sushmita Sen (1994) and Ms. Lara Dutta (2000).

CHAPTER TWENTY-FOUR

Corona Is Back - Omicron - 2022 Corona Version

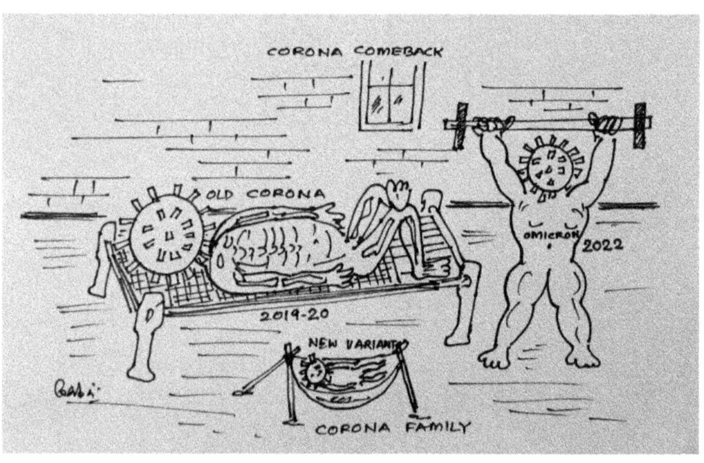

Omicron - 2022 Corona Version

This cartoon was sketched on 10 January, 2022. Corona made its comeback in a new mutated form, "Omicron". The whole world is infected by Omicron virus. In India, its peak has been forecasted to hit around mid of February, 2022.

CHAPTER TWENTY-FIVE

Flames Merging

Merging of two flames

This was sketched on 21 January 2022. On 21 January 2022 (Friday), flame of India Gate's Amar Jawan Jyoti was merged with the flame at the National War Memorial at New Delhi. Merging of flames is said to be an attempt to delink India's colonial past.

CHAPTER TWENTY-SIX

Union Budget 2022 - Bringing Digital Rupee

Union Budget 2022 - bringing digital Rupee

This was sketched on 1 February, 2022. In a big 'no' to the crypto currencies, Digital Rupee will be introduced in India during the 2022 - 23 financial year, Finance Minister, Government of India Ms. Nirmala Sitharaman said while presenting the Union Budget 2022. The Reserve Bank of India has stated that it will soon begin working towards the phased implementation of country's own digital currency. While presenting Budget 2022-23, Finance Minister also said that the transfer of digital assets, including crypto and non-fungible tokens (NFTs), will be subject to a 30% tax. Even gifting such assets will result in a 30% tax.

CHAPTER TWENTY-SEVEN

Russia - Ukraine War

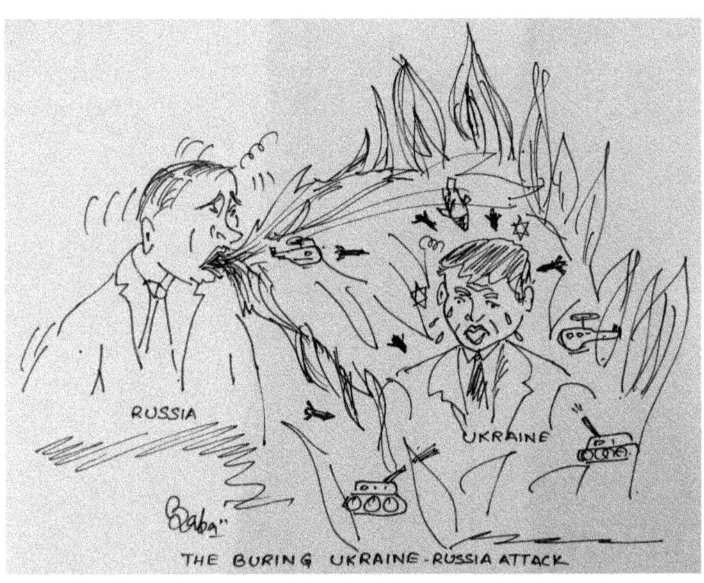

Russian blitzkrieg on Ukraine

This was sketched on 1 March, 2022. On 24 February, 2022, Russia began a large military invasion of Ukraine. Ukraine is a country, which borders south-western Russia. This Russia - Ukrain war marks a steep escalation of a conflict that began in year 2014. Russian blitzkrieg is the largest conventional military attack in Europe since World War II.

CHAPTER TWENTY-EIGHT

2022 States Assembly Elections In India

2022 States Assembly elections In India

This cartoon was sketched on 11 March, 2022. BJP had a landslide victory in four states viz. Uttar Pradesh, Uttarakhand, Goa and Manipur. For the first time in the history of Uttar Pradesh and Uttarakhand, after successful completion of full five years, some party had again come for power, in succession. AAP had a landslide victory in the state of Punjab.

CHAPTER TWENTY-NINE

Dramatic Change Of Prime Minister In Pakistan

Dramatic change of Prime Minister in Pakistan

This cartoon was sketched on 10 April, 2022. Pakistani opposition political parties have passed the no-confidence vote in parliament seeking the ouster of Prime Minister Imran Khan, in a high political drama, largely on accusations of gross economic mismanagement. As many as 174 members recorded their votes in favour of the resolution. Now, Mr. Shehbaz Sharif is the new Prime Minister of Pakistan since 11 April 2022.

CHAPTER THIRTY

Need Of Religious Tolerance And Brotherhood In India

Need of religious tolerance and brotherhood in India

This was sketched on 17 April 2022. A massive violent clash on 16 April 2022 evening broke out in Delhi's Jahangirpuri area during a Hanuman Jayanti procession, leaving many people injured. The incident took place during 'Shobha Yatra' that was being taken out by the devotees of Lord Hanuman, when some people allegedly said to be from other religion, started pelting stones on the procession. Many vehicles were torched, and policemen were injured. Similar incidents were also reported from other Indian states of Madhya Pradesh and Rajasthan, and few other places. There is a need of religious tolerance, mutual respect, trust and brotherhood. India is the land of Ram, Krishna, Buddha, Mahavira, Nanak, Kabira, Meera, Dadu, saints and sages and other many enlightened souls, which taught love, respect and peace for their whole life.

CHAPTER THIRTY-ONE

High Voltage Drama In Maharashtra

Eknath Shinde rebels with 40 Member of Legislative Assembly of Shiv Sena

This cartoon was sketched on 30 June, 2022. Eknath Shinde had defected with almost 40 MLAs of Shiv Sena, the ruling party in the state of Maharashtra in India. He toppled the government. Eknath Shinde claimed that he has 50 Member of Legislative Assembly (MLA) with him, including 40 MLAs from Shiv Sena. It lead to the debacle of the party, and created a serious political crisis in the state of Maharashtra. Later, Eknath Shinde made the government and took the charge of the Chief Minister of Mahashtra with the support of Bhartiya Janta Party (BJP) on 30 June, 2022. After almost 10 days of high-octane scramble for power, Maharashtra finally got a new government consisting of BJP and Shiv Sena's rebel faction led by Eknath Shinde. It brought an an end to a 10 days of political turmoil and the high voltage drama in the state. Further, Bharatiya Janata Party (BJP) leader Devendra Fadnavis took oath as the Deputy Chief Minister.

CHAPTER THIRTY-TWO

A Phenomenal Journey

A phenomenal journey

Droupadi Murmu became 15th President of India on 25 July, 2022. She was born on 20 June, 1958. She is the first tribal, second woman, and the youngest President of India born post-independence. She was ninth Governor of Jharkhand state in India between years 2015 and 2021. She had held various portfolios in Government of Odisha between years 2000 to 2004. She had worked as a clerk in Odisha State Irrigation and Power Department between years 1979 to 1983. Later, she became teacher in Rairangpur until 1997. In 1997, Droupadi Murmu was elected as the Councillor of the Rairangpur Nagar Panchayat in Odisha, which was a reserved seat for a woman, as the independent candidate.

CHAPTER THIRTY-THREE

India Celebrates 75th Anniversary Of Its Independence

India celebrates 75th anniversary of its independence

This was sketched on 15 August, 2022. India celebrated its 75th anniversary of independence on 15 August, 2022. It was named as, "Azadi Ka Amrit Mahotsav". "Har Ghar Tiranga" i.e. India's tricolour national flag on every house, campaign was also launched. "Azadi Ka Amrit Mahotsav" was an initiative of the Government of India. It was aimed at celebrating and commemorating 75 years of independence and the glorious history of its people, culture and achievements. This Mahotsav activated "India 2.0", which was fuelled by the spirit of Aatmanirbhar Bharat. Various celebrations of "Azadi Ka Amrit Mahotsav" commenced on 12th March 2021, which started a 75-week countdown to 75th anniversary of independence, and will end post a year on 15th August, 2023.

CHAPTER THIRTY-FOUR

A New Dawn - INS Vikrant

A new dawn - INS Vikrant

This was sketched on 5 September, 2022. INS Vikrant is the first indigenous and largest ship made by India, which includes indigenous designs and aircraft carriers for the Indian Navy. INS Vikrant is a significant milestone achieved by the country on the basis of the Aatmanirbhar Bharat

Campaign. INS Vikrant was launched at Cochin Shipyard Limited (CSL) on 2 September, 2022. Now with its launch, India comes under the elite nations, where it owns its giant power ship. The name is derived from India's first aircraft carrier, which was used in the war against Pakistan in the year 1971.

CHAPTER THIRTY-FIVE

Cheetah Diplomacy

Cheetah Diplomacy

This cartoon was sketched on 17 September, 2022. Eight cheetahs from Namibia arrived in India on 17 September, 2022, as per Cheetah Conservation Fund (CCF). The big cats were released into India's Kuno National Park in the state of Madhya Pradesh. Eight Cheetahs, five of which are female, were flown from Windhoek, Namibia to Gwalior, followed by a helicopter ride to the grasslands of Kuno, Palpur in Madhya Pradesh.

CHAPTER THIRTY-SIX

Light Combat Helicopter "Prachand"

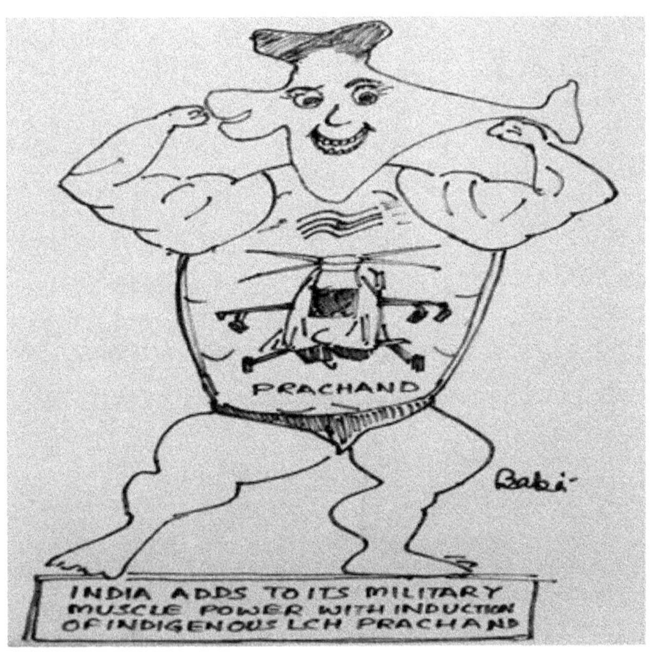

Light Combat Helicopter (LCH) "Prachand"

This cartoon was sketched on 10 October, 2022. The indigenously developed Light Combat Helicopter (LCH) "Prachand", meaning fierce, was formally inducted into the Indian Air Force at the Jodhpur Airbase on 10 October, 2022 (Monday). Prachand has been designed, developed and extensively test-flown for over a decade by Hindustan Aeronautics Ltd (HAL). Prachand is a multi-role attack helicopter. Prachand has been customised as per the requirements of the Indian armed forces to operate both in desert terrains and high-altitude sectors. Prachand is the only attack helicopter in the world, which can land and take off at an altitude of 5,000 metres (16,400 ft.). Prachand is also capable of firing a range of air-to-ground and air-to-air missiles.

CHAPTER THIRTY-SEVEN

India Gets G20 Summit 2023 Presidency

India gets G20 Summit presidency for the year 2023

This cartoon was sketched on 17 November, 2022. The 17th Group of Twenty (G20) Heads of State and Government Summit took place in October 2022 in Bali, Indonesia under the Indonesian Presidency. G20, 2022 focussed on the theme, 'Recover Together, Recover Stronger'. The 2023 G20 Delhi Summit is the upcoming eighteenth meeting of Group of Twenty (G20), a Summit scheduled to take place in Pragati Maidan, New Delhi in the year 2023. India's presidency began on 1 December, 2022, leading up to the Summit in the fourth quarter of 2023.

CHAPTER THIRTY-EIGHT

FIFA World Cup Qatar 2022

FIFA World Cup Qatar 2022

This cartoon was sketched on 21 November, 2022. The 2022 FIFA World Cup is 22nd FIFA World Cup. It is being hosted in Qatar from 20 November up to 18 December,

2022. It is the first World Cup, being hosted in the Arab, and second to be hosted fully in the Asia. This will be the last World Cup with 32 teams. Next World Cups are going to have 48 teams. The tournament is being played in November and December as Qatar is a very hot country. This is the first World Cup that isn't played in May, June or July. The previous champions are France. FIFA is much awaited, and spectated sports events in the world, having maximum fans.

CHAPTER THIRTY-NINE

India China Troops Clash Tawang Arunachal Pradesh

India China troops clash at Tawang in Arunachal Pradesh

This cartoon was sketched on 13 December, 2022. India - China troops clash took place at Tawang in Arunchal Pradesh on 9 December, 2022. China is trying to alter status quo along the Line of Actual Control (LAC) for many years. Around 300-400 soldiers from People's Liberation Army (PLA) of China had intruded across LAC. This intrusion by PLA was contested by the Indian soldiers in a very firm and resolute manner, ultimately forcing the Chinese soldiers to retreat. It was first such encounter, after deadly Galwan valley incident, which had taken place in June 2020.

CHAPTER FORTY

Joshimath Land Subsidence

Joshimath land subsidence

This was sketched on 14 January, 2023. Joshimath in the state of Uttarakhand in India is sinking. The exact reasons behind the Joshimath land subsidence are still unknown, however experts are citing unplanned construction, over-population, obstruction of the natural flow of water, and the hydel power activities as possible causes of this land subsidence. Cracks have appeared in many roads, and in hundreds of houses of Joshimath. Joshimath is a seismic zone, which makes it prone to frequent earthquakes.

CHAPTER FORTY-ONE

MV Ganga Vilas Cruise

MV Ganga Vilas Cruise

This cartoon was sketched on 13 January, 2023. It was a historic moment, when Indian Prime Minister had flagged off the world's longest river cruise, MV Ganga Vilas. This cruise will cover 3,200 kilometres across 27 river systems, passing through five states in India, and the Bangladesh, in 51 days. The "Made-in-India" vessel began its journey from Varanasi in the state of Uttar Pradesh in India and will reach Dibrugarh in the state of Assam in India via

Bangladesh.

CHAPTER FORTY-TWO

Bharat Jodo Yatra Of Indian National Congress

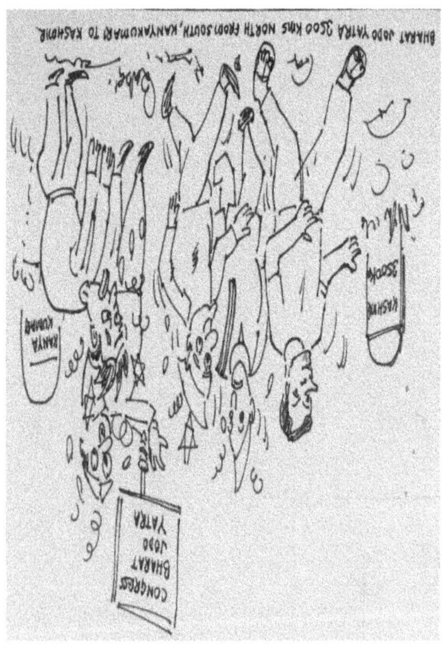

Bharat Jodo Yatra of Indian National Congress

This cartoon was sketched on 30 January, 2023. Bharat Jodo Yatra (Unite India March) was a mass movement led by Mr. Rahul Gandhi of Indian National Congress (INC). It was a Padayatra (journey by foot or hiking) of 146 days. Bharat Jodo Yatra, a political and social movement, was a protest by INC against divisive policies and actions of the government. Bharat Jodo Yatra aimed at upholding unity of India. Bharat Jodo Yatra had started on 07 September, 2022 from the city of Kanyakumari in the state of Tamil Nadu in India, and had ended on 30 January, 2023 at Srinagar in Jammu & Kashmir in India. Bharat Jodo Yatra had covered total 4,080 kilometres.

CHAPTER FORTY-THREE

Hindenburg Report On Adani Group

Hindenburg Report on Adani Group

This cartoon was sketched on 30 January, 2023. Hindenburg Report disclosed that it holds short positions in Adani Group through U.S. traded bonds and non-Indian-traded derivatives. Hindenburg Report alleges Adani Group of improper use of tax havens, and flagged concerns about Group's debt levels. Adani Group shares started plummeting due to these imposed allegations by the Hindenburg Report.

CHAPTER FORTY-FOUR

Maharaja Of Skies

Maharaja of skies - Tata's Air India

This cartoon was sketched on 14 February, 2023. The Tata group-owned Air India has placed the largest ever aircraft order in global aviation history with Letter of Intent (LoI) being signed for purchase of 470 aircrafts, which will be a mix of narrow body and wide body Airbus, and Boeing aircrafts. Before it, in year 2011, American Airlines had placed an order for 460 aircrafts.

CHAPTER FORTY-FIVE

India Shines Bright At Oscars 2023

India shines bright at Oscars 2023

This cartoon was sketched on 14 March, 2023. India shines bright at Oscars 2023. For the first time, two Indian films have been awarded Oscars in the 95th Oscar Awards, India wins "The Best Documentary Short" for 'The Elephant Whispers', and "The Best Original Song Award" for RRR's 'Naatu Naatu'.

CHAPTER FORTY-SIX

Rahul Gandhi Expelled From Indian Parliament

Rahul Gandhi expelled from Indian Parliament

This cartoon was sketched on 29 March, 2023. Rahul Gandhi, leader of India's Congress Party, and the Indian opposition leader has been expelled from the Parliament, 24 hours after he was convicted of defamation for a remark implying that Prime Minister, Narendra Modi was a criminal. Also, Rahul Gandhi has been sentenced to two years in prison.

CHAPTER FORTY-SEVEN

Wrestlers Protest In India

Wrestlers protest in India

This cartoon was sketched on 8 May, 2023. Woman wrestlers organized a sit-in at Jantar Mantar, New Delhi, earlier in January 2023, making the sexual harassment allegations against Mr. Brij Bhushan Sharan Singh, Chief of

Wrestling Federation of India (WFI) and BJP Member of Parliament. Delhi Police has filed FIRs based on complaints of seven woman wrestlers, including a minor one, alleging sexual harassment and criminal intimidation.

CHAPTER FORTY-EIGHT

Former Pakistani Prime Minister Mr. Imran Khan Arrested

Former Pakistani Prime Minister Mr. Imran Khan arrested by NAB

This cartoon was sketched on 9 May, 2023. On 9 May, 2023, former Pakistani Prime Minister and politician Mr. Imran Khan was arrested from inside the High Court at Islamabad by National Accountability Bureau (NAB). There are charges of corruption on Mr. Khan in connection with his Al-Qadir Trust, which he owns alongside his wife Ms. Bushra Bibi. Following Mr. Khan's arrest by NAB, his party Pakistan Tehreek-e-Insaf called for nationwide demonstrations.

CHAPTER FORTY-NINE

India - USA GE 414 Jet Engine Deal

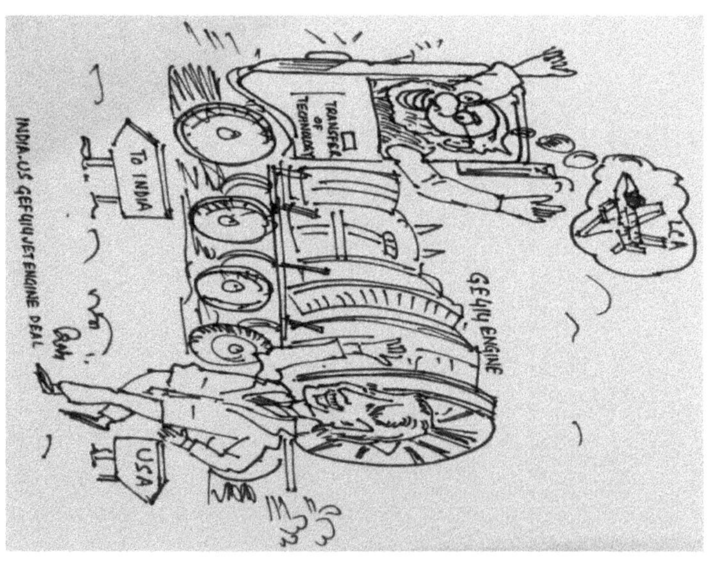

India - USA GE 414 Jet Engine Deal

This cartoon was sketched on 25 June, 2023. This Deal for Transfer of Technology (ToT) was signed during India's

Prime Minster visit to USA on 22 June, 2023. General Electric (GE) Aerospace and Hindustan Aeronautics Limited (HAL) have signed a Memorandum of Understanding (MoU) to co-produce fighter jet engines for Light Combat Aircraft (LCA) Tejas MK - 2 for the Indian Air Force (IAF).

CHAPTER FIFTY

Launch Of Chandrayaan - 3 Spacecraft

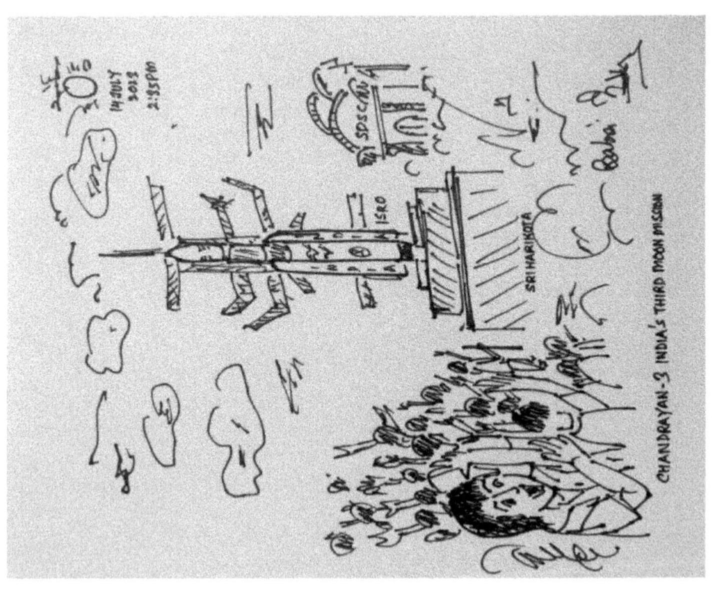

Launch of Chandrayaan - 3 spacecraft

This illustration was sketched on 15 July, 2023. Indian Space Research Organisation (ISRO) Chandrayaan - 3 spacecraft was successfully launched onboard Launch Vehicle Mark - 3 (LVM3) on 14 July, 2023 at 2:35 PM from Satish Dhawan Space Centre - Sriharikota Range (SHAR), Sriharikota, Tirupati District, State of Andhra Pradesh in India. Its mass is 3900 Kgs.. Its landing date at Moon is 23 August, 2023. Chandrayaan - 3 is third edition of India's Moon Mission.

CHAPTER FIFTY-ONE

India's Chandrayaan - 3 Lands On The Moon

India's Chandrayaan - 3 lands on the Moon

This illustration was sketched on 24 August, 2023. Indian Space Research Organisation (ISRO) Chandrayaan - 3 spacecraft had smoothly and successfully landed on

Moon at India's time 6 : 04 PM on 24 August, 2023. India became first country to land on the South Pole of Moon, and fourth to land on the Moon, after USA, Russia and China. Chandrayaan - 3 is third edition of India's Moon Mission. India's Chandrayaan - 3 Rover will explore the lunar surface and collect invaluable scientific data.

CHAPTER FIFTY-TWO

India In 19th Asian Games 2023

India in 19th Asian Games 2023

This was sketched on 9 October, 2023. The 19th Asian Games were held at Hangzhou in the People's Republic of China from 23 September, 2023 to 8 October, 2023. The India had sent 655 athletes to compete in 41 disciplines at the 19th Asian Games 2023. The India had finished fourth in the overall medals tally at the 19th Asian Games 2023, with total 107 Medals, i.e. 28 Gold Medals, 38 Silver Medals, and 41 Bronze Medals. It was the India's best-ever medal haul at the quadrennial event. The People's Republic of China had stood First with total 383 Medals. The Japan had stood Second with total 188 Medals. And, the Republic of Korea stood Third with total 190 Medals. The multi-sport event was hosted by the Olympic Council of Asia (OCA), which brought together the top athletes from different countries of the Asian continent.

CHAPTER FIFTY-THREE

2023 Israel - Hamas War; Explosion In Al-Ahli Arab Hospital

2023 Israel - Hamas War; Explosion in Al-Ahli Arab Hospital

This was sketched on 18 October, 2023. An armed conflict had started between the Hamas-led Palestinian militant groups and the Israeli military forces on 7 October, 2023. Hamas attacked the southern Israel, codenamed it "Al-Aqsa Flood", which had killed 1,400 Israelis. Israeli military forces conducted a heavy retaliatory blitz against Palestine's Gaza Strip, and killed more than 8,000 Palestinians. On 17 October 2023, an explosion took place in the parking lot of the courtyard of Al-Ahli Arab Hospital in Gaza City of southwestern Palestine, resulting in more than 500 fatalities and several injuries among displaced Palestinians seeking shelter there. The Israeli Military says the explosion, one of the deadliest attacks on a hospital in decades, was the result of a misfired Palestinian Islamic Jihad rocket. The massive killing at Al-Ahli Arab Hospital has spurred a very widespread international condemnation, followed by protests at the Israeli Embassies in several countries.

CHAPTER FIFTY-FOUR

The 2023 Uttarakhand Tunnel Collapse

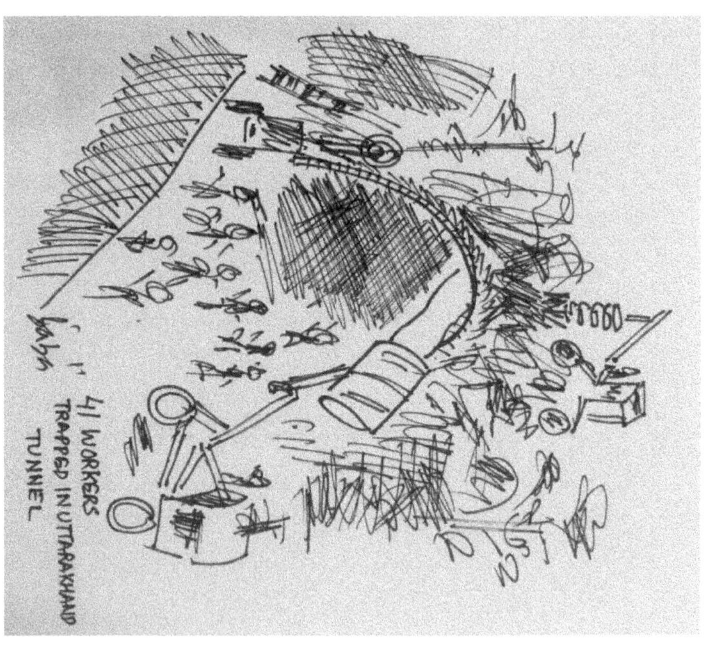

The 2023 Uttarakhand tunnel collapse

This was sketched on 13 November, 2023. The 2023 Uttarakhand tunnel collapse had occurred on 12 November, 2023. A landslide had triggered, portion of the under construction Silkyara - Barkot tunnel, in the Uttarkashi district of the state of Uttarakhand in India, to collapse, and thus trapping 41 workers, approximately 200 meters from the entrance of the tunnel. The tunnel collapse had occurred at around 5:30 AM IST, and thus trapping total 41 workers inside the tunnel. After being trapped for 17 days inside the tunnel, all 41 trapped workers were finally been rescued by the efforts of multiple - agencies including the Indian Army, especially the Rat Miners, on 28 November, 2023 (Tuesday). The team of 24 Rat Miners had started their work on 27 November, 2023 (Monday) to drill through the debris pile manually. They created a narrow passageway to the trapped men. Each trapped worker was pulled out individually on a wheeled stretcher. The healths of all 41 workers were medically examined, and were found to be fine.

CHAPTER FIFTY-FIVE

Indian Assembly Election Results December 2023

Indian Assembly Election Results December 2023

This was sketched on 04 December, 2023. Bhartiya Janta Party (BJP) led by Mr. Narendra Modi, Prime Minister of India, had won assembly elections of Indian states of Madhya Pradesh (MP), Rajasthan and Chattisgarh with thumping margins. Indian National Congress led by Mr. Rahul Gandhi could only manage to win the Indian state of Telangana. Zoram People's Movement (ZPM) has won the assembly elections of Indian state of Mizoram. These assembly elections are being considered as the precursor to the next General Elections, expected to be held in India, between April 2024 and May 2024, to elect the members of the India's 18th Lok Sabha.

Books By Dr. Yaduvir Singh

To laugh is to love the self. Cartoons are the instruments for laughter, and bring inner peace. Laughter keeps the beings positive and healthy. Happiness is the requirement of the Soul. Happiness is necessary for experiencing the God. A bestselling Cartoon Book, published by Dr. Yaduvir Singh in year 2021 is, "2020 & 2021 - The Cartoon Book".

Other best-sellers (Books) on Life Engineering (Spirituality) genre by Dr. Yaduvir Singh are, "Pyramid - Spiritual Journey Companion", "The Secret of Happiness", "Beyond the Blood, "Power of Positive Thinking", "Becoming Rich", "Power of Subconscious Mind", "The Ghost", "Tere Bina - Without You", "Experiencing the God", "Himalaya - The Spiritual Abode", "Death - Demystified", and "Life - A Continuous Journey".

All these Books are very easily available on e-commerce platforms Amazon, Flipkart and Others, and Bookstores.

www.ingramcontent.com/pod-product-compliance
Lightning Source LLC
LaVergne TN
LVHW021140160826
845679LV00023B/1988